TASTE THE WORLD!

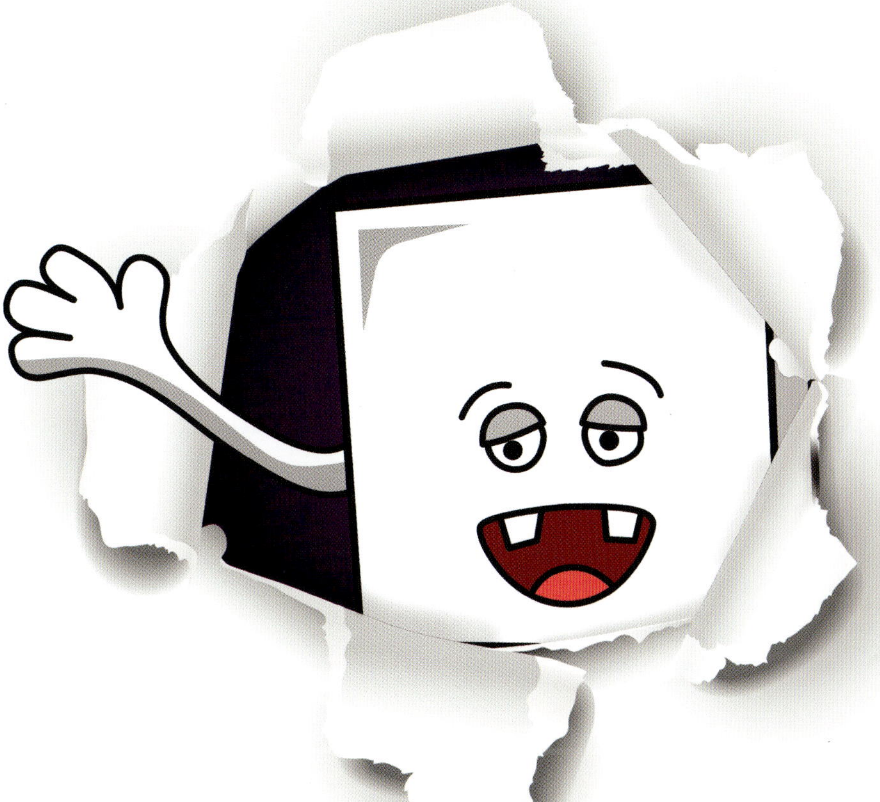

SUGAR

www.worldbook.com

TABLE OF CONTENTS

4 I Am Sugar!
6 What Is Sugar?
8 A Closer Look at Sugar Cane and Sugar Beets
10 SOUTH PACIFIC

11 PHILIPPINES

12 A Sweet Rivalry: Australia vs. New Zealand

14 INDIA
16 Other Sweet Sources

18 CHINA
20 Rock Candy on a Stick
22 Types of Sugar

24 MIDDLE EAST
26 NETHERLANDS
28 ISLANDS IN THE ATLANTIC
30 CARIBBEAN
32 Sugar Meets Savory

34 BRAZIL

36 GERMANY

37 FRANCE
38 A Sweet Sight!

40 RUSSIA

42 UNITED STATES

44 Sweet Temptation!
46 Glossary/Helpful Hints
47 Index
48 Acknowledgments

BEFORE YOU BEGIN

Included in this book are a few recipes that allow you to "taste the world!" Before you begin, look on page 46 for some helpful hints. Read the recipes carefully and always ask an adult to help—especially when handling knives or using the stove. Besides, cooking is easier and more fun when you work together!

I AM SUGAR!

As we travel around the world, we'll explore my history, discover some fun facts, and learn to prepare some delicious recipes. Along the way, you may read words that are new to you. If I can explain what a word means easily, I'll do it right where you are reading. If I use the word many times, or if the explanation is complicated, I will put the word in **boldface** (type that **looks like this**). Boldface words are defined in a glossary in the back of the book.

WHAT IS SUGAR?

Sugar is a food used to make other foods sweet. It can be sprinkled on strawberries or added to sweeten lemonade. Some foods, such as ice cream, jam, cookies, and candy, are made with sugar. Other foods that are not even sweet—like bread and peanut butter—contain sugar. Since ancient times sugar has been around, in one form or another, throughout the world!

FAR OUT!

Sugar has been found in meteorites and in an interstellar gas cloud in the Milky Way!

I've been around!

All green plants—think fruits and vegetables—make sugar. This common sugar is called **sucrose** or table sugar. Sugar cane and sugar beets are important sources of sucrose. The sugar that comes from these plants is the kind that people keep in a sugar bowl.

DID YOU KNOW that foods contain other kinds of sugar? In addition to sucrose, fruits and vegetables contain fructose. Glucose is found in both plant and animal foods. Milk and cheese contain lactose. Nuts and grains contain maltose. Sugar belongs to the group of foods called **carbohydrates.** Carbohydrates provide energy to plants and animals—including people! Sugar tastes good, but eating too much of it is not good for our health.

A CLOSER LOOK AT SUGAR CANE...

Sugar cane is a tall grass that thrives in tropical and semitropical climates. Sugar cane stores sucrose in its stalks. These fibrous stalks grow 7 to 30 feet (2 to 9 meters) high and about 2 inches (5 centimeters) across.

After sugar cane stalks are harvested, they are crushed, soaked, and squeezed to release sweet juice. The juice is then boiled to evaporate water, leaving a thick syrup. The syrup is then spun in a machine. When the syrup is spun at very high speeds, sugar crystals separate from the syrup, producing raw sugar. This sugar is tan in color.

To make pure white sugar for table use, the raw sugar must be rinsed, filtered, spun, and dried.

SWEET JUICE

Nearly 90 percent of the weight of the cane is juice. This juice contains up to 17 percent sucrose.

...AND SUGAR BEETS

Sugar beets grow in *temperate* climates, where the days are warm and the nights are cool. The long, pointed white roots weigh from 1½ to 3 pounds (0.7 to 1.4 kilograms). About 15 to 20 percent of this weight is sucrose.

After harvesting, the sugar beet root is washed, sliced, and soaked to release the juice. The juice is filtered and the water is removed, producing a thick syrup. The syrup is spun and dried to produce *granular* (grains of) sugar.

Sugar is a terrible thing to waste!

UNTAPPED SWEETNESS

People in ancient Babylon, Egypt, and Greece grew sugar beets for their leaves. They ate them like spinach or chard. They didn't yet know how sweet beets could be!

ROOT

CANE BEATS BEETS!

About 80 percent of sugar comes from sugar cane; 20 percent comes from sugar beets.

MORE THAN 8,000 YEARS AGO, PEOPLE GREW SUGAR CANE ON THE ISLANDS OF THE

SOUTH PACIFIC

The people of New Guinea were most likely the first to grow sugar cane. New Guinea is a large tropical island in the Pacific Ocean, north of Australia. Originally people chewed the raw sugar cane to enjoy its sweetness. They did not know yet how to *extract* (squeeze out) sugar from the cane. Today, sugar cane is an important crop for the South Pacific islands.

DID YOU KNOW that chewing on sugar cane is healthier for you than eating the sugar crystals? Sugar cane has important minerals and vitamins that are removed during the production of sugar from the cane.

There are many islands in the South Pacific. Each island has its own distinct culture. But their **cuisines** share some European, American, and Asian influences. On the island of Fiji, a sugar pudding called *pudini* is a favorite. It may have been introduced by the British. Regardless of where a recipe comes from, food plays an important role in the lives of the islanders. It represents community and generosity. A visitor will always be asked to share a meal.

RAISE THE FLAG!

Sugar cane is so important to Fiji that it appears on the country's flag.

SUGAR CANE MADE ITS WAY TO THE

PHILIPPINES

The Philippines is an island country of more than 7,000 islands. Sugar cane is raised for local use and for export. The country's hot, humid climate is ideal for raising cane... and for enjoying such cold sweet treats as *halo-halo*!

NO MOO? NO PROBLEM!

Few dairy cows are raised in the Philippines. So to make a cool dessert like ice cream, other ingredients are cleverly used in place of milk!

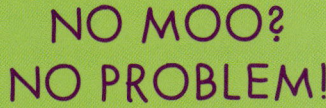

Hello, halo-halo!

Halo-halo is a colorful Filipino dessert. Translated as *mix-mix*, it is both chewy and crunchy! Halo halo is made with shaved ice topped with sweetened **condensed milk** and such ingredients as *ube* (purple yam), *kaong* (sugary palm fruit), sweet beans, coconut gel, lychees, tapioca pearls, and *pinipig* (crunchy rice flakes). Use your imagination, *mix-mix*, and enjoy!

A SWEET RIVALRY: AUSTRALIA vs. NEW ZEALAND

Australia and New Zealand have argued for years over who deserves credit for inventing the much-loved dessert *pavlova*. Pavlova is a sweet, snowy-white cake that is marshmallowy on the inside and crunchy on the outside. The cake is made by beating egg whites with sugar into a thick foam called **meringue.** After the cake is baked, it is covered with whipped cream and fruits. It is a sweet way to celebrate holidays and special occasions.

May I have this dance?

TUTU PRETTY!
Whichever country created pavlova, everyone can agree that it was named for the famous Russian ballerina Anna Pavlova. This is because it looks like a white *tutu* (ballerina skirt)!

SUGAR ADDS STRUCTURE!

It is the sugar in the pavlova that allows the meringue to hold its shape and keep its height. Without sugar, the cake would collapse. As the batter is beaten, air is added to the mixture, creating volume. The sugar bonds to the water molecules in the eggs and acts like glue to hold the foamy mixture together.

SUGAR CANE WAS ALSO GROWN IN ANCIENT

INDIA

India's tropical climate is perfect for growing sugar cane. India is considered the birthplace of crystallized sugar. More than 1,600 years ago, the people of India figured out a way to turn the sugar cane stalks into sugar granules. This process made it possible for sugar to be easily traded.

Sugar is one of the ingredients in **chutney.** Chutney is a jam-like *condiment* (topping) that adds extra flavor to foods. It is served with almost every meal in India. Chutney is made with fruits or vegetables that are cooked with sugar and seasoned with spices. It makes a great topping for *chapati,* an Indian flatbread!

I don't mind getting into a jam!

SHARKARA

The word sugar originates from the Sanskrit (ancient Indian language) word *sharkara,* which means *material in a granule form.*

SUGAR IS A PRESERVATIVE!

Sugar can be used to preserve fruit. When fruit is cooked with sugar, much of the water in the fruit is replaced with sugar. Without water, germs cannot grow and spoil the fruit. By cooking the fruit with sugar, the fruit can last longer!

 Turn some fresh strawberries into a tasty treat for your toast!

STRAWBERRY JAM   Makes 2 cups

INGREDIENTS

2 cups fresh strawberries, washed and chopped with hulls and stems removed

¾ cup sugar

2 tbsp. fresh lemon juice

STEPS

1. HAVE AN ADULT cook the strawberries, sugar, and lemon juice in a saucepan over medium-high heat, mashing the strawberries while stirring. Cook until bubbles cover the surface of the jam, about 10 minutes. The jam is ready when the consistency is like a thick maple syrup or the temperature reaches 220 °F (104 °C).
2. Let cool and spoon into a container with a lid. It will keep in the refrigerator for 2 weeks.

DID YOU KNOW that sailors took jam on their voyages to keep them from getting sick? On long voyages, they needed vitamin C, which they were able to get by eating the preserved fruit.

15

COOKING WITH
OTHER SWEET SOURCES

There are other sources of sweetness besides table sugar. When using these ingredients in recipes, they provide a different taste and texture than sugar. Here are some sweet suggestions...

HONEY

is our oldest known sweetener. It is a thick fluid made by bees from flower **nectar,** a sugar-filled liquid. Honey is 25 to 50 percent sweeter than sugar and has a distinctive flavor. Baked goods made with honey (like these honey buns) are moist and dense, and tend to brown faster than those made with granulated sugar.

FLOWER POWER!

There are over 300 kinds of honey. The color and flavor of honey depend on the kinds of flowers that supply the nectar that the bee drank!

Let the sweets compete!

MAPLE SYRUP

comes from the **sap** of maple trees. The sap is a colorless, watery liquid. People boil it into a dark, sticky syrup. People pour maple syrup on pancakes and waffles, and manufacturers use it to flavor candies. It also makes a tasty glaze for foods like carrots!

MOLASSES

is made from the material left over from the sugar-making process. It contains only about 50 percent sugar, so it is less sweet. Molasses works well with such savory dishes as baked beans and barbecue sauce. Adding molasses to cookie batter adds moistness and chewiness to these ginger snaps!

CANDY BOOGERS?!

Sundot kulangot (picked boogers) is a Filipino candy made with coconut jam and molasses. The sticky candy is enclosed in wooden balls. It got its name because you use your finger to pick the candy out of the ball!

GROWING AND REFINING SUGAR CANE
SPREAD EAST FROM INDIA TO

CHINA

Sugar became a common ingredient of Chinese food around the A.D. 600's. It still is today! Rock sugar is often used in Chinese cuisine. Guangdong Province in southeastern China is famous for rock sugar. Rock sugar is a gold-colored sugar that comes in irregular lumps. The crystals can be up to an inch (2 ½ centimeters) wide. You need to break up the crystals to use them in recipes. Rock sugar has a pleasant taste, with no caramel tones. It is not as sweet as table sugar. Rock sugar is used in tea, desserts, soups, sauces, stir fries, and to *marinate* (soak) meat.

Today, China is a leading producer of both sugar cane and sugar beets.

How sweet it is!

SWEET!

One of the five basic Chinese tastes is "sweet." This is called *kan* in Chinese. The other tastes are sour, salty, pungent, and bitter.

DID YOU KNOW that painting with caramelized sugar is a tasty Chinese tradition? Sugar is melted over a fiery pot and spread over a marble slab with a spoon. Dragons, birds, fish, and monkeys are popular designs.

CARAMELIZING DEEPENS COLOR AND FLAVOR!

As sugar gets hot, it undergoes a chemical reaction called **caramelization.** In this process, sugar molecules break down into smaller and smaller parts. The sugar turns a deep shade of brown and develops a more complex flavor. Caramelized rock sugar is used to marinate such classic Chinese dishes as braised pork belly. The process allows the pork to brown better while cooking as it takes on a mouth-watering glazed look.

HOW TO MAKE
ROCK CANDY ON A STICK

Now that you have learned about rock sugar, here is a fun way to make a candy treat—rock sugar on a stick!

How it works: When you mix hot water and sugar, the water can only hold the sugar if both stay very hot. As the hot water cools and evaporates, the sugar comes out of the liquid and is left behind. Watch over the next few days as sugar crystals grow slowly on the stick! Add food coloring for dazzling and delicious rock candy!

JUST ADD WATER

Candy is made by dissolving sugar in water. Different heating levels determine the types of candy: Hot temperatures make hard candy, medium temperatures make soft candy, and cool temperatures make chewy candy.

Rock on!

TRY THIS!

This recipe uses very hot liquid. HAVE AN ADULT HELP YOU with it for safe and tasty fun!

ROCK CANDY

INGREDIENTS

narrow jar or glass
wooden skewer (or clean wooden chopstick)
clothespin

1 cup water
2-3 cups sugar
food coloring (optional)

STEPS

1. Clip the skewer into the middle of the clothespin. Then position the clothespin so that each end rests atop the rim of the glass and the skewer hangs down inside the glass. The bottom of the skewer should be about 1 inch (2.5 cm) from the bottom of the glass. If the skewer is too long, cut the bottom to this length with scissors. Remove the skewer and clothespin and put them aside for now.
2. HAVE AN ADULT pour the water into a pan and bring it to boil on a stove.
3. Turn off the heat. Add 1 tablespoon of sugar in the boiling water and stir until it dissolves.
4. Continue adding sugar, 1 tablespoon at a time, letting each tablespoonful dissolve completely before adding the next. Add food coloring if desired, according to directions.
5. When no more sugar will dissolve in the water, allow the solution to cool.
6. While the sugar solution cools, dip the lower half of the skewer into the solution, then roll it in some sugar. Let the skewer cool completely.
7. Pour the cooled sugar water into the glass.
8. Position the clothespin back atop the rim of the glass, making sure that the attached skewer is submerged in the glass and that it is hanging straight down the middle without touching the sides of the glass.
9. Allow the glass and skewer to sit in a warm place without being disturbed for several days until the water evaporates. As the water evaporates, it will leave sugar crystals on the skewer. Enjoy your rock candy!

A LOOK AT SOME COMMON
TYPES OF SUGAR

There are many different types of sugar. They play different roles in cooking and baking. Here are the types of sugar most commonly used in recipes.

GRANULATED SUGAR

is the most common kind sold. It comes in the form of white granules. It adds sweetness and moisture to baked goods and helps them brown while baking. Granulated sugar makes pastries tender and gives crunch to some types of cookies.

TRY THIS!

White sugar is the star of this classic recipe! These soft, chewy, sparkly cookies can be enjoyed during the holidays or anytime!

SUGAR SPARKLE COOKIES
Makes 4 dozen

INGREDIENTS

- 2 ¾ cups all-purpose flour
- 1 tsp. baking soda
- ½ tsp. baking powder
- 1 cup butter, softened
- 1 ½ cups white sugar, plus an extra bowl of sugar for rolling
- 1 egg
- 1 tsp. vanilla extract

STEPS

1. Stir together flour, baking soda, and baking powder in a small bowl. Set aside.
2. In a large bowl, beat together the butter and sugar until smooth and creamy. Beat in egg and vanilla. Gradually blend in the dry ingredients. Roll rounded teaspoonfuls of dough into balls. Roll cookies in the bowl of sugar to coat. Place onto cookie sheets lined with parchment paper.
3. Bake 8 to 10 minutes in a 375 °F (190 °C) preheated oven, or until golden. Let stand on cookie sheet two minutes before removing to cool on wire racks.

"One lump or two?"

BROWN SUGAR,

whether light or dark, is a mixture of molasses syrup and sugar. Dark brown sugar has more molasses and a deeper, richer flavor than light brown sugar. Brown sugar is often used in baking. It makes a rich and moist streusel crumb topping for pies, muffins, and cakes.

CUE THE CUBE!

A Swiss-born director of a sugar beet refinery in what is now the Czech Republic invented the single-serve sugar cube in 1843. Before that, people used a *sugar nipper* (a pair of sharp-edged pincers) to cut sugar from a loaf for tea. They dunked the chunk of sugar in their tea and reused it!

POWDERED SUGAR

(also called *confectioners' sugar*) is 10 times finer than granulated sugar. It is made by grinding granulated sugar to a fine powder. It is then mixed with a small amount of cornstarch to prevent clumping. Powdered sugar is preferred for icings and candy because it dissolves very easily. It is also used as a decorative dusting for baked goods.

23

INDIA SPREAD ITS KNOWLEDGE OF SUGAR PRODUCTION TO THE

MIDDLE EAST

The Middle East is a region across southwestern Asia and northeastern Africa. There, Arab chemists figured out how to improve the sugar manufacturing process. People in the Middle East eagerly adopted sugar into their cuisine. They made products with sugar that delighted everyone who tasted them. Beginning in the 600's A.D., Arab culture spread, often through trade. Wherever the Arabs went, they brought sugar with them.

Egypt began refining sugar cane in 710. The sugar industry is one of the oldest in Egypt. Today, both sugar cane and sugar beets are important crops in Egypt.

Turkey, a country that lies both in Europe and in Asia, is also a major producer of sugar beets today.

"HONEY WITHOUT BEES"

Historians believe that Darius I, the ruler of the Persian Empire, introduced sugar cane to the Middle East. In 510 B.C., he invaded India, where he found "the reed which gives honey without bees" and brought it back to his homeland.

"Delightful!"

DID YOU KNOW that **Turkish delight** is one of the oldest sweets in the world? Legend has it that 500 years ago, a Turkish sultan ordered his cooks to make a unique dish for him. The result was *lokum,* or Turkish delight, a jellylike candy made of sugar, water, gelatin, and flavoring. Traditional varieties are often flavored with rosewater, orange, or lemon, and may be filled with anything from fruit to pistachios. The popular candy has been a part of Turkish culture for centuries!

SWEET INSPIRATION

Spanish painter Pablo Picasso ate Turkish delight every day to help concentrate on his work. French Emperor Napoleon I and the British statesman Winston Churchill enjoyed Turkish delight with pistachio filling.

EUROPE GETS INTO THE SUGAR TRADE, INCLUDING THE

NETHERLANDS

By 636, sugar cane had made its way from the Middle East to Europe. But sugar was an expensive import that only the wealthy could afford. In the 1400's, Spanish and Portuguese explorers began conquering lands where they planted sugar cane. In the 1600's, the Dutch got into the act. Sugar production and trade helped the Netherlands prosper during its "Golden Age."

The Dutch are known for their love of sweets in such foods as pancakes and breads. The Netherlands is the third largest consumer of sugar. Today, the Dutch grow their own sugar in the form of sugar beets, one of the country's chief products.

SUGAR GIVES DOUGH A LIFT!

Adding sugar to a yeast dough will make it rise faster. The sugar feeds the yeast, causing it to grow. Because sugar will absorb some of the water in the dough, breads made with yeast will turn out more soft and tender. Sugar will also help in making a nice crusty brown top.

I'll help you make some dough!

26

The Dutch make this soft sweet bread with swirls of cinnamon-coated chunks of sugar baked right in! This loaf is delicious and easy to make. It is best served slightly warm with butter.

SUIKERBROOD (SUGAR BREAD)

Makes 1 loaf

INGREDIENTS

- 1 ¼ cups whole milk, lukewarm
- 2 tbsp. white sugar, divided
- 1 (0.25 ounce) package active dry yeast
- 1 egg
- 2 ¾ cups all-purpose flour
- 1 tsp. salt
- 2 ½ tbsp. butter
- 2 tsp. vegetable oil, divided
- ¾ cup Belgian pearl sugar or sugar cubes that have been smashed into small pieces
- 1 tsp. ground cinnamon

STEPS

1. Mix 1 tablespoon of sugar with the yeast in a small bowl. Stir in the warm milk until dissolved. Let it stand in a warm dark place for about 10 minutes until it becomes frothy. Make sure the milk is lukewarm. If it is too hot, it will kill the yeast and the bread will not rise.
2. In a small bowl, whisk the egg and reserve 1 tablespoon in a separate bowl. This reserve will be used later.
3. Melt 1 ½ tablespoons of butter. In a large bowl, sift the flour and stir in the salt. Make a well in the flour and add the yeast mixture, beaten egg, and melted butter. Stir until all the ingredients are combined. Transfer the dough to lightly floured work surface and knead for about 10 minutes. The dough should have a smooth and elastic texture.
4. Coat a large bowl with 1 teaspoon of oil. Place the dough in the bowl and turn the dough so that it gets a coating of the oil. Cover the bowl with plastic cling film and a towel. Let it stand in a warm place for about an hour or until it is doubled in size.
5. Melt 1 tablespoon of butter. In a medium bowl, combine the butter with the pearl or sugar cube pieces and the cinnamon.
6. Place the risen dough on a lightly floured work surface and form it into a rectangle. Dot the dough with half of the sugar pieces and knead until incorporated. Repeat this step to incorporate the remaining sugar pieces.
7. With the remaining oil, grease a 9 x 5 ½ x 3-inch loaf pan. Sprinkle remaining sugar all over the pan to cover the sides and the bottom.
8. Shape the dough into a rectangle one more time and fold each side to the center to form a loaf. Place the dough in the loaf pan with the seam on the bottom. Using a damp cloth, cover the bread pan and let it rise for about 30 minutes.
9. Preheat oven to 375 °F (190 °C). Gently remove the damp cloth from the pan and brush the top of the dough with the remaining whisked egg.
10. Bake until top is golden brown and a toothpick comes out clean, about 35 to 45 minutes. Cool in the pan for about 10 minutes and remove the bread from the pan. Let the bread cool a bit more before slicing.

EUROPEANS PLANTED SUGAR CANE IN NORTHERN AFRICA AND ON

ISLANDS IN THE ATLANTIC

One of these places was the Canary Islands, a group of 13 islands in the Atlantic Ocean off the northwest coast of the mainland of Africa. The islands belong to Spain.

A typical Canarian dessert is *bienmesabe*, from the island of La Palma. It is made from almonds, eggs, sugar, and lemon. Its name is Spanish for "It tastes good to me!"

CANARY CUISINE

The cuisine of the Canary Islands is a mixture of Spanish, African, and Latin American foods, as well as some native *Guanche* elements. The Guanches are the islands' original inhabitants. Historians believe they originally came to the islands from North Africa.

Portuguese settlers developed sugar cane plantations on the Madeira Islands around 1425. These volcanic islands lie in the Atlantic Ocean off the northwest coast of Africa. Sugar cane is still a chief crop on the Madeira Islands. The islands belong to Portugal today.

At Christmastime, Canarians love their *trucha* (trout) for dessert! This traditional dessert is a dumpling stuffed with sweet potato and almonds and sprinkled with sugar. It got its name from its fishlike shape!

JUST A SPOONFUL OF SUGAR...

When sugar arrived in Europe, it was rare and precious. People thought of it as a medicine. It was often sold by druggists, who used it to flavor bad-tasting medicines.

ENGLISH, FRENCH, AND DUTCH COLONIZERS BROUGHT SUGAR CANE TO AMERICA AND THE

CARIBBEAN

The Caribbean Islands, sometimes called the "sugar islands," divide the Caribbean Sea from the Atlantic Ocean. Here in 1515, English colonists built the first **sugar mill** in the Western Hemisphere. By the 1700's, sugar cane from the Caribbean was traded all over the world. Sugar made so much money that traders called it "white gold"!

CARIBBEAN CANE

In 1493, the Italian navigator Christopher Columbus brought sugar-cane cuttings to islands in the Caribbean. Sugar cane is the region's leading crop today.

Caribbean cuisine is a mixture of African, Creole, Cajun, Native American, European, Latin American, East and North Indian, Middle Eastern, and Chinese foods. There are also dishes that are unique to the region.

DID YOU KNOW that the word **jerk** comes from the Spanish word *charqui,* meaning *jerked* or *dried meat?* The word comes from Quechua, the language of the Inca of South America. Jerk is a style of cooking native to Jamaica. It can refer to a spice *rub* (mixture), marinade, or cooking technique.

You'd be a jerk not to try it!

SUGAR THICKENS SAUCES!

Adding a little bit of sugar to such sauces as Jamaican jerk sweet potato and black bean curry will help make the liquid less runny. The sugar in the liquid gives the sauce a smoother, thicker texture.

MORE THAN JUST FOR DESSERT
SUGAR MEETS SAVORY

Sugar is not just for desserts and candy! Small amounts can be added to savory foods to balance flavors. Added to sauces, sugar gives a boost of flavor with a surprise hint of sweetness.

Asian cuisines make use of sugar in many dishes, including Korean *galbi jjim* (braised short ribs); Chinese plum and garlicy *hoisin* dipping sauces for dumplings like *dim sum* or potstickers; Thai tamarind sauce for *pad thai* noodles; Thai/Vietnamese Sriracha sauce for dipping seafood or with Vietnamese *pho* noodle soup; and Japan's *teriyaki* marinade for grilled meat or fish.

SWEET SAUCE

Maraqat halwa is an Algerian sauce made from butter and seasoned with cinnamon, saffron, and honey or sugar. It is often served with lamb.

SUGAR BALANCES ACIDIC FOODS!

Sauces made with vinegar—including barbecue sauce, German *sauerbraten* marinade, and Italian tomato sauce—have a high acid content. Adding a bit of sugar will neutralize acidity and give the sauce a smooth, bright flavor.

Barbecue sauce may have global origins, but it has become an American staple. It often uses such sweet ingredients as brown sugar, which thickens the sauce and adds a delicious caramel flavor. Many regions of the United States pride themselves on their unique barbecue sauces, including northern Alabama; Kansas City and St. Louis, Missouri; Memphis, Tennessee; North Carolina; Santa Maria Valley, California; and Texas.

PORTUGUESE COLONISTS PLANTED SUGAR CANE IN BRAZIL

Portuguese colonists established large sugar cane plantations in northeastern Brazil in the 1500's. Brazilian sugar brought great wealth to Portugal. Today Brazil leads the world in sugar cane production and is a top exporter of raw sugar.

Fresh sugar cane juice is popular with Brazilians at farmers' markets called *feiras*. Brazilians also often nibble *goiabada*, a sugary, thickened guava paste. Guava is a tropical fruit.

FUDGING FUDGE!

Brigadeiro is a traditional Brazilian dessert similar to a fudge ball. It is made of sweetened condensed milk, cocoa powder, eggs, and butter, then rolled in chocolate sprinkles. Brigadeiros are a popular treat for birthdays, served along with the cake.

Mmmmm! Thanks, Chocolate!

SUGAR MAKES A CAKE LIGHT AND TENDER!

Many cakes, even birthday cakes, will benefit from adding some sugar. A light, tender cake crumb is achieved by creaming butter with sugar. The hard surface of the sugar creates air pockets in the batter. When the batter is baked, these air pockets expand, producing a light, fluffy, and tender cake crumb.

FINDING ANOTHER WAY TO MAKE SUGAR IN

GERMANY

Back in Europe, sugar cane remained an expensive import. But in 1747, a German chemist found that sugar from the sugar beet was the same as sugar from cane! It wasn't until 1799, when a practical method of removing sugar from sugar beets was invented, that sugar became more affordable and available to most Europeans.

ZUCKER is the German word for *sugar*.

I'm a sucker for *zucker!*

DID YOU KNOW that a pinch of sugar can take away a bitter flavor? Schwäbischer Kartoffelsalat, a traditional potato salad made in Swabia, a land in southwest Germany, adds a little sugar to its vinegar-based dressing. The sugar helps reduce the bitter flavor but still allows the tang of the vinegar to come through.

SUGAR BEETS IN
FRANCE

Today, France is the second largest producer of sugar beets. It began in the 1800's, when Emperor Napoleon I decreed that 79,000 acres (32,000 hectares) of land was to be used solely for the growing of sugar beets.

DID YOU KNOW that sugar heated to a high temperature will melt? That is how the sugary crust of crème brûlée is made. Crème brûlée is a French favorite. Break the hard sugar crust to reveal the soft creamy custard below. Scoop and enjoy!

C'est si bon! (It's so good!)

BE SWEET TO DONKEYS

In the village of Saint-Léger-des-Prés, it is illegal to insult a donkey. If you do, you must apologize with sugar cubes!

DECORATING WITH SUGAR IS
A SWEET SIGHT!

Sugar plays many roles in the culinary world because it is so versatile! Decorating with sugar creates a feast for the eyes!

Caramelized sugar in liquid form can be drizzled into shapes. When it cools, it hardens.

EYE CANDY!

Cake decorating began in Europe in the mid-1600's. Elaborate cakes were displayed at feasts and banquets in the homes of wealthy people. In the mid-1800's, the French began to serve decorated desserts as a sweet course after the meal.

Marzipan is a moldable confection made of sugar and ground-up almonds. It can be colored and flavored. Marzipan is often used to decorate cakes. It is chewy and sweet to eat!

DID YOU KNOW that sugar can be molded into shapes? During the Mexican holiday *Día de los muertos (Day of the Dead)*, people make treats from sugar that are shaped like skulls to honor the dead. The skulls are made from molds and brightly painted.

A sweet feast for the eyes!

A simple slice of bread spread with butter becomes "fairy bread" when it is sprinkled with *nonpareils*—tiny balls made with sugar and starch. Fairy bread is a special treat served in Australia.

SUGAR BEETS BECOME A TOP CROP IN RUSSIA

Russians eat a lot of sugar! Doughnuts, sweetened condensed milk, ice cream, and pancakes filled with jam are all favorites made with sugar. In the 1600's, before the country turned to sugar beets, Russia imported great amounts of cane sugar from Egypt.

All that imported sugar cost a lot of money. So Russia began growing its own sugar from sugar beets in the 1800's. Today, Russia is the largest producer of sugar beets.

When it comes to sugar, you can't beet Russia!

A soft, melt-in-your-mouth Russian treat is called *zefir*. It is similar to **marshmallow**. Zefir is made with sugar, pureed apple, and egg whites. It is named after Zephyr, the Greek god of the light west wind, because of its delicate, airy consistency.

TRY THIS!

All you need is a little gelatin to turn sugar into fluffy marshmallows! HAVE AN ADULT HELP YOU WITH THIS RECIPE: Very hot liquids and a sharp knife are used. You will also need a candy thermometer.

FLUFFY MARSHMALLOWS

INGREDIENTS

Makes 20-40 marshmallows

2 envelopes unflavored gelatin
1/3 cup cold water
1 1/2 cups sugar
1/4 cup water
1/4 cup corn syrup
1/2 tsp. vanilla extract
cooking spray
confectioners' sugar

STEPS

1. Line a 9-inch x 13-inch baking pan with foil. Use several sheets of foil to cover both the length and the width of the pan. Let the edges hang over by a few inches. Lightly spray the foil with cooking spray.
2. Put 1/3 cup of water into the bowl of an electric mixer. Sprinkle the gelatin on top of the water. Let sit for at least 15 minutes.
3. In a saucepan, whisk the sugar, 1/4 cup of water, and corn syrup over medium heat. Once the sugar is dissolved, stop whisking. HAVE AN ADULT heat the mixture until it boils and place a candy thermometer into the saucepan. Turn off the stove when the mixture reaches 240 °F (115 °C).
4. HAVE AN ADULT carefully pour the hot liquid over the gelatin. Beat on high speed for 10 to 12 minutes until the liquid is opaque and expands to fill the bowl. Mix in the vanilla extract.
5. Using a rubber spatula, quickly scrape the marshmallow mixture into the prepared pan.
6. Cover the pan with plastic wrap and let it set overnight, or 12 to 15 hours.
7. Remove the plastic wrap, pull the foil-wrapped marshmallow out of the pan, lay the marshmallow on the cutting board, and peel off the foil.
8. HAVE AN ADULT cut the marshmallow into 1-inch-wide strips. Then cut the strips into cubes.

DID YOU KNOW that when sugar is heated to its boiling point it will harden like a lollipop when cooled? Adding corn syrup lowers the boiling point, creating a softer, fluffier marshmallow.

FROM EGYPT, WITH LOVE

Ancient Egyptians were the first to enjoy the gooey treat we call marshmallow as early as 2000 B.C.

SUGAR PRODUCTION CATCHES UP IN THE
UNITED STATES

Sugar experts from the Caribbean helped establish cane sugar in Louisiana. In 1791, the first sugar mill on the North American mainland was built in New Orleans. Today, Louisiana is one of the leading producers of cane sugar in the United States. The United States ranks fifth of all countries in sugar cane production.

Nothing says "American dessert" like apple pie! Top it off with ice cream and a sweet **caramel** sauce. Caramel is made by heating sugar to a high temperature. The amber-colored mixture is then combined with cream. *Yummmmmm!*

SUGAR BOWL

Sugar is such a big deal in Louisiana that there is a sporting event named in honor of it! Since 1935, New Orleans has hosted the annual Sugar Bowl college football game.

DID YOU KNOW that caramel was first made by the Arabs around 950?

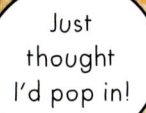

Just thought I'd pop in!

TRY THIS!

Use a microwave oven to make this quick and tasty caramel corn!

CARAMEL CORN

Serves 4

INGREDIENTS
- 2 regular bags unflavored, low-sodium microwave popcorn, popped
- ½ cup butter
- 1 cup dark brown sugar
- ¼ cup light corn syrup
- ½ tsp. salt
- ½ tsp. baking soda

STEPS
1. Place popped, cooled popcorn in a large paper bag.
2. Place butter, brown sugar, corn syrup, and salt in a large microwavable glass bowl and microwave for 1 minute on high. Remove from microwave and stir.
3. Return mixture to microwave and cook on high for an additional 2 minutes. Remove from microwave and stir in the baking soda. Be careful when adding the baking soda: it will foam up. When all the ingredients are incorporated, pour it over the popcorn in the paper bag. Quickly close the bag and shake well.
4. Microwave the closed bag for 1 ½ minutes. Take it out of the microwave and shake. Return the bag to the microwave, flip over, and cook for an additional 1 ½ minutes. Remove and shake well. Flip the bag again and cook for 45 seconds more. Remove and shake again. Popcorn is very hot: use mitts to flip and shake the bag.
5. Place the popcorn on an ungreased cookie sheet and allow it to cool.

Thanks, Corn!

Beet sugar was first produced in the United States in Northhampton, Massachusetts, in 1838. The country's first successful sugar-beet processing factory was built in 1870 in Alvarado, California, near Oakland.

Today, the United States is the third largest producer of sugar beets. The Red River Valley in Minnesota and North Dakota is the largest sugar-beet growing region in the United States.

RESISTING SWEET TEMPTATION!

Although sugar is a sweet treat that is hard to resist, it should be eaten in small amounts. A little bit of sugar is nice in many foods, but too much is not good for your health. It is not good for people's teeth, and it can cause a person to gain too much weight. Eat a well-balanced diet to avoid sweet surrender!

CRAVINGS!

Sweet cravings are associated with skipping meals. Sweet treats should not replace a meal!

WHAT MAKES A WELL-BALANCED DIET?

People who study nutrition say that each day people should eat a certain number of servings from each of five food groups. The five food groups include: breads, cereals, rice, and pasta (such as macaroni and spaghetti); vegetables; fruits; milk, yogurt, and cheese; and meat, poultry (chicken and turkey), fish, dried beans and peas, eggs, and nuts. Different people need different amounts of servings from each food group. Children, adults, older people, and women who are going to have a baby all have different needs.

Watch that sweet tooth!

GLOSSARY

caramel *(KAR uh muhl, KAHR muhl)* Sugar browned or burned and used for coloring and flavoring food.

caramelize *(KAR uh muh lyz, KAHR muh)* To melt sugar over heat so that it turns brown.

carbohydrate *(KAHR boh HY drayt)* Carbohydrates are made up of carbon, hydrogen, and oxygen. Sugar and starch are carbohydrates.

chutney *(CHUHT nee)* A spicy sauce or relish made of fruits, herbs, pepper, and other seasoning.

cuisine *(kwih ZEEN)* A style of cooking or preparing food.

condensed milk (also called **sweetened condensed milk**) A thick, sweetened milk prepared by evaporating some of the water from whole milk and sweetening it.

jerk *(jurk)* To preserve meat by cutting it into long, thin slices and drying it in the sun.

marshmallow *(MAHRSH MAL oh, -MEHL-)* A soft, white, spongy candy, covered with powdered sugar. It is made from corn syrup, sugar, starch, and gelatin.

marzipan *(MAHR zuh pan)* A confection made of ground almonds and sugar, molded into various forms.

meringue *(muh RANG)* A mixture made of egg whites beaten stiff and sweetened with sugar, often flavored.

nectar *(NEHK tuhr)* A sweet liquid found in many flowers.

sap *(sap)* The liquid that circulates through a plant, consisting of water and food.

sucrose *(SOO krohs)* The chemical name for common table sugar.

sugar mill A machine or factory for making sugar, as by pressing the juice out of sugar cane.

Turkish delight A jellylike candy made, usually in cubes dusted with powdered sugar, of sugar, water, gelatin, and flavoring.

Parting is such sweet sorrow!

HELPFUL HINTS

When working in the kitchen with food, keep these helpful hints in mind to make sure your work goes smoothly and safely. Then enjoy the tasty treats you make!

- **Wash your hands** before you begin food preparation and after you've touched raw eggs or meat.
- Thoroughly **wash fruits and vegetables.**
- **Use oven mitts** when handling hot pots, pans, or trays.
- **Have an adult help** when working with knives and hot stoves or ovens.

INDEX

acidic foods, 33
Australia, 12-13, 39

barbecue sauce, 17, 33
bienmesabe, 28
Brazil, 34-35
bread, 26-27, 39
brigadeiro, 34
brown sugar, 23

cakes, 12-13, 34-35, 38
Canary Islands, 28-29
candy, 17, 20-21, 38-39
caramel, 42-43
caramel corn (recipe), 43
caramelization, 19, 38
carbohydrates, 7
Caribbean Islands, 30-31, 42
China, 18-19
chutney, 14
Columbus, Christopher, 30
crème brûlée, 37

Darius I, 24

Egypt, 24, 40-41

Fiji, 10
France, 37, 38
fructose, 7

Germany, 36
glucose, 7
granulated sugar, 22

halo-halo, 11
honey, 16

India, 14

Jamaica, 31
jerk, 31

lactose, 7
Louisiana, 42

maltose, 7
maple syrup, 17
maraqat halwa, 32
marshmallows, 40
   recipe, 41
marzipan, 38
meringue, 12-13
Mexico, 39
Middle East, 24-25
molasses, 17, 23

Napoleon I, 25, 37
nectar, 16
Netherlands, 26-27
New Guinea, 10
New Zealand, 12-13
nonpareils, 39

pavlova, 12-13
Philippines, 11, 17
Portugal, 28, 34
powdered sugar, 23
pudini, 10

rock candy, 20
   recipe, 21
rock sugar, 18-20
Russia, 40-41

sauces, 17, 31-33
Schwäbischer Kartoffelsalat, 36
South Pacific Islands, 10
strawberry jam (recipe), 15
sucrose, 7, 8

sugar, 4-7
   as preservative, 15
   decorating with, 19, 38-39
   in diet, 44-45
   savory food with, 32-33
   substitutes for, 16-17
   types of, 22-23
sugar beets, 7, 9
   in China, 18
   in Europe, 26, 36, 37
   in Middle East, 24
   in Russia, 40
   in United States, 43
sugar cane, 7-9
   in Atlantic islands, 28
   in Brazil, 34
   in Caribbean, 30
   in China, 18
   in Europe, 26, 36
   in India, 14
   in Middle East, 24
   in Philippines, 11
   in South Pacific Islands, 10
   in United States, 42
sugar cookies (recipe), 22
sugar cubes, 23, 37
sugar mills, 30, 42
suikerbrood (recipe), 27
sundot kulangot, 17

trucha, 29
Turkey, 24, 25
Turkish delight, 25

United States, 33, 42-43

yeast, 26

zefir, 40

47

World Book, Inc.
180 North LaSalle Street
Suite 900
Chicago, Illinois 60601
USA

Copyright © 2020 (print and e-book) World Book, Inc.
All rights reserved.

This volume may not be reproduced in whole or in part in any form without prior written permission from the publisher.

WORLD BOOK and the GLOBE DEVICE are registered trademarks or trademarks of World Book, Inc.

For information about other "Taste the World!" titles, as well as other World Book print and digital publications, please go to www.worldbook.com.

For information about other World Book publications, call 1-800-WORLDBK (967-5325).

For information about sales to schools and libraries, call 1-800-975-3250 (United States) or 1-800-837-5365 (Canada).

Library of Congress Cataloging-in-Publication Data for this volume has been applied for.

Taste the World!
ISBN: 978-0-7166-2858-3 (set, hc.)

Sugar
ISBN: 978-0-7166-2865-1 (hc.)

Also available as:
ISBN: 978-0-7166-2873-6 (e-book)

Printed in China by RR Donnelley, Guangdong Province
1st printing July 2019

STAFF

Editorial

Writer
Shawn Brennan

Manager, New Product Development
Nick Kilzer

Proofreader
Nathalie Strassheim

Manager, Contracts and Compliance (Rights and Permissions)
Loranne K. Shields

Manager, Indexing Services
David Pofelski

Digital

Director, Digital Product Development
Erika Meller

Digital Product Manager
Jonathan Wills

Graphics and Design

Coordinator, Design Development and Production
Brenda Tropinski

Senior Visual Communications Designer
Melanie Bender

Media Editor
Rosalia Bledsoe

Senior Web Designer/Digital Media Developer
Matt Carrington

Manufacturing/Production

Manufacturing Manager
Anne Fritzinger

Production Specialist
Curley Hunter

ACKNOWLEDGMENTS

Cover © Brent Hofacker, Shutterstock; © BT Photo/Shutterstock; © Andrea Leone, Shutterstock; © Marcos Mesa Sam Wordley, Shutterstock

Character artwork by Matthew Carrington

- 2-3 © Shutterstock; Sgt. Richard DeWitt, U.S. Army
- 4-9 © Shutterstock
- 10-11 Sgt. Richard DeWitt, U.S. Army; © Hendrasu/Shutterstock
- 12-19 © Shutterstock
- 20-21 © BT Photo/Shutterstock; © xMarshall/Shutterstock; WORLD BOOK photo by Brenda Tropinski
- 22-23 © Stock image/Shutterstock; © Africa Studio/Shutterstock; © Kvitka Fabian, Shutterstock; © Anjelika Gretskaia, Getty Images
- 24-29 © Shutterstock
- 30-31 © Eric Laudonien, Shutterstock; © Stacy Grant, StockFood
- 32-33 © Stephanie Frey, Shutterstock; © Matt Johannsson, StockFood; © Sevenke/Shutterstock
- 34-37 © Shutterstock
- 38-39 © Graham Montanari, Shutterstock; © Bernhard Winkelmann, age footstock; © Marie Charouzova, Shutterstock; © Drferry/iStockphoto; © Brent Hofacker, Shutterstock
- 40-41 Public Domain; © Brent Hofacker, Shutterstock
- 42-45 © Shutterstock

Thanks for coming along!

48